For

Krystyna
Sebik

ELENIKA
SKOLIKOVA
00 4/21 3-7
7 92493

10 PM Samm
3PM here?

Pearls
of Wisdom

By
Beth Mende Conny

Illustrated by
Jo Gershman

PETER PAUPER PRESS, INC.
WHITE PLAINS, NEW YORK

To Aunt Jersey

Copyright © 1996
Peter Pauper Press, Inc.
202 Mamaroneck Avenue
White Plains, NY 10601
ISBN 0-88088-801-6
Printed in China
14 13 12 11 10 9 8

Introduction

*Experience can teach only
what you are willing to learn.*

Life offers many lessons. May these pearls
of wisdom offer you the opportunity to
reflect and celebrate, to enjoy and grow.

B. M. C.

A journey begins not with
the first step but with the
desire to go where you
have never gone.

*I*n the game of love, there
should always be two winners.

*W*hen opportunity knocks,
don't just stand there.
Open the door!

*W*ishing won't make it so,
but it's not a bad place
to begin.

*W*hen we love, we see
with our hearts.

*C*hoose your words carefully,
for they define who you are.

*T*rust others, but not
before yourself.

*S*hould a door slam in
your face, open a window.

*R*eal education begins with
the willingness to learn
from mistakes.

*I*f all the world's a stage and
we are all players, there's no
need for stage fright.

*I*f you can't find a way, make one.

*T*o find the right answer, you
must ask the right question.

*W*hen you sail the sea of change, it's natural to long for shore.

*W*hen you open your heart,
you open your mind.

*A*ll things come to
those who wait—
but not indefinitely.

*I*t's not enough to know
how to do something;
you must also know
why it should be done.

*L*ife is full of simple pleasures—
long walks, good books, soft
kisses, and delicious chocolates.

*T*he present is the future you
envisioned for yourself long ago.

*S*et an example—for yourself.

A risk a day helps keep
your fears away.

A goal is a way station on
the road of life.

*T*o give and receive are,
ultimately, the same.

*W*hy all the rush to find yourself
when you are here, now?

*W*ith each choice you
consciously make, you learn
to trust yourself.

*F*ace the light and you'll
never see shadows.

*T*o truly love others,
give them the space to
love themselves.

*D*iscover the power of
positive thinking—surround
yourself with positive thinkers.

*L*ife is a grand mystery with
an infinite number of clues.

*F*ate is often what you
most secretly desire.

*L*ife is a creative act and each
day a potential masterpiece.

*L*uck chooses those who
are prepared.

*T*he most precious gift you
give another is your time
and attention.

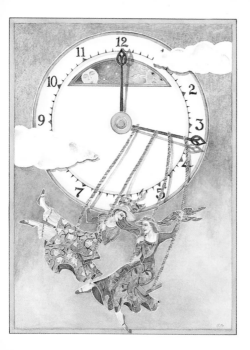

*W*hen you can't do what you
would like, do what you can.

*P*atience often takes
patience to learn.

*W*hen you give with love,
not expectation, you receive
more than you ever
thought possible.

*T*he more you fill your life
with anger, the less room
there is for love.

*F*ailure is opportunity
in disguise.

*Y*ou are who you are,
not who you used to be.

Solitude is the soil in which
your true self blossoms.

*F*aith and drive are an
unbeatable twosome.

*W*hen you put your problems
into words, you also put
them into perspective.

*Y*ou learn self-discipline
when you tell yourself "no."

A 24-karat friend makes
every day golden.

*F*aith is the first rung of
any ladder you climb.

*A*void the great temptation—
settling for too little in your life.

*T*o soar through life, you must
take yourself off autopilot.

*D*on't reject what you
know little about.

*W*hen you find work you
love, you no longer have to
work for a living.

*C*ourage is being able to
look to yourself, not others,
to solve your problems.

*T*o love is to listen.

*A*dopt an open door policy—
let in new ideas and experiences.

*L*ife is not a dress rehearsal
but a live production.

*Y*our loved ones are the
threads who weave the
fabric of your life.

*W*e may sail in different
directions, but we're all
in the same boat.

*W*hen you quiet your
mind, you truly hear.

*L*et others know what
you stand for—and what
you won't stand for.

*S*ay your piece, then
make your peace.

*K*indness is a language that
fills the air with song.

*T*ake a firm stand—to be flexible.

*G*entleness often is a
sign of strength.

*F*orgiveness is a miracle worker.

When you're on the right track, joy travels with you.

*F*orget perfection—there is
always something you can
do better.

*W*hen people say you can't,
turn the other ear.

*M*ake your heart a home
into which you invite loving
thoughts and friends.

*E*xperience can teach only
what you are willing to learn.

*W*ith faith you are never alone.